Second Nature

Winner, 23rd Annual A. Poulin Jr. Poetry Prize

Selected by Matthew Shenoda

Second Nature

Chaun Ballard

*

Foreword by Matthew Shenoda

New Poets of America Series No. 55

BOA Editions, Ltd. * Rochester, NY * 2025

First Edition
23 24 25 26 7 6 5 4 3 2 1

For information about permission to reuse any material from this book, please contact The Permissions Company at www.permissionscompany.com or e-mail permdude@gmail.com.

Publications by BOA Editions, Ltd.—a not-for-profit corporation under section 501 (c) (3) of the United States Internal Revenue Code—are made possible with funds from a variety of sources, including public funds from the Literature Program of the National Endowment for the Arts; the New York State Council on the Arts, a state agency; and the County of Monroe, NY. Private funding sources include the Max and Marian Farash Charitable Foundation; the Mary S. Mulligan Charitable Trust; the Rochester Area Community Foundation; the Ames Amzalak Memorial Trust in memory of Henry Ames, Semon Amzalak, and Dan Amzalak; and contributions from many individuals nationwide. See Colophon on page 124 for special individual acknowledgments.

Cover Art and Design: Sandy Knight
Interior Design and Composition: Isabella Madeira
BOA Logo: Mirko

BOA Editions books are available electronically through BookShare, an online distributor offering Large-Print, Braille, Multimedia Audio Book, and Dyslexic formats, as well as through e-readers that feature text to speech capabilities.

Cataloging-in-Publication Data is available from the Library of Congress.

BOA Editions, Ltd.
250 North Goodman Street, Suite 306
Rochester, NY 14607
www.boaeditions.org
A. Poulin, Jr., Founder (1938-1996)

Contents

III.

Foreword

What you hold in your hands is a collection of poems that braids together the unencumbered memories of family lineage and African American history. Chaun Ballard explores what it means to be shaped by others, to make a way in the world carrying the pieces of the imperfect men and women who brought us to this moment. Ballard's poems speak to the idea of a continuum, articulating the life of the poet on his own terms without forgetfulness or a simple investment in the fragmented lie of the individual. These are poems of community and history, of the collision of time, of what it means to live in ancestry and in the particulars of place.

Second Nature is driven by an intergenerational rhythmic impulse that finds its music in both the daily living and the ever-existing stories of family and kin, community and place. The poems found here weave themselves into the landscapes and antecedents of culture and spark the imaginations of memory and imagery, of song and sorrow. Ballard's poems are tactile and attendant to the overarching realities of Black life, to the ways that history and the present shape everything we know to be. He takes his power from the everyday of those he calls *his*. The impulse here is not to simply tell an individual story, but to forever cast the self in the inextricable entanglement of those we come from and those we go with. As Ballard writes:

> Because living is hard work. Especially, when every piece of legislation is meant to uproot you. &,
> at the heart of every grass root, is a movement of bees fighting to keep. Which is a statement. &
> believe me, I understand the effort it takes to show. & not explain.

In this vein Ballard takes the *whole* as his domain and as a result this book becomes a refusal; a refusal of singularity, a refusal to cast Black life under the spotlight of a single lamp. These poems enact a quiet and revolutionary insistence that many things are true at once, that the light and shade of life is cast and illuminated from many places, at many angles, and that he and we can be more than what we have been made to believe. He celebrates, no matter the moment, the capacity of simple acts and like any poet worth their salt he gives due to the things most would ignore:

> Our neighborhood of stolen bikes, backyards, & so-
> called conditions of standard living (where nothing was much),
> Papa would drive up, reverse, & parallel into his spot like the spot depends
> on the smoothness of his return.

It is moments like the one above where Ballard's true poetic positionality comes into clear view, his recognition that power exists in these intimate and ordinary moments, that the archives of Black life are not in grand institutions or earth shattering acts, but in the personal moments that shape our memories, that carve the paths of our continuums, that each of us steal away to make our own marks, however small, on the world around us. In this way, every poem collected here relies on a dependence of others in order to come into full existence. The poet is never separated from those he holds dear:

> & speaking of fire, my buddy returns home from the years he tallied upstate. &, even I, if I may venture a tad off course— to enter into the weeds, am tempted to call his return to "civility" *freedom.* But the true freedom is not in my naming him *returned,* but how my friend emerges from a front door that he unlatches himself

Each of Ballard's poems attempts that kind of unlatching, that kind of simple gesture that marks us towards freedom by the very fact of its being. In these persistent small acts, these moments that feel like "second nature," we prove our living, and it is that very living that makes an indelible mark on the world.

Throughout the collection Ballard leads us from the tenuous but persistent relationship with his father, the stories and words of his grandmother, the boyhood dreams of basketball and the music that populate his life, to the overarching laws and histories that have shaped America and the searing ever-presence of the landscape he walks on; Ballard steadily reminds us of the both/and, the beauty and the struggle, never severing the space between them, or as he reminds us:

> beauty is the birthplace of a heartache

—Matthew Shenoda

Everything that happened…involved music. It was part of every day life, as automatic as breathing.

Nina Simone

I do believe that something went wrong, somewhere.

I'm asking what's come…over me. I've changed, I've been changed.

Let me tell you something about myself.

Johnnie Taylor

A Poem Ending with a Strambotto wherein I Include an Extra Line That Is Myself *or* A Poem in which I Name the Flower

I think back to the words of the geo-spatial engineer,
      sitting next to my wife & myself in a bar, who shared
with a curious neighbor about the renewing nature
      of fire. How, when it comes to fire, it is healthy
for the land to set itself against itself. For context,
      I am not speaking of country. Currently, I am speaking
of fire. & speaking of fire, my buddy returns home from
      the years he tallied upstate. &, even I, if I may venture
a tad off course, to enter into the weeds, am tempted
      to call his return to "civility" *freedom.* But the true
freedom is not in my naming him *returned,* but how
      my friend emerges from a front door that he unlatches
himself, to record what grows freely in the absence
      of one man. & like that, it is dandelion season again.

A resident weed of every state. & my favorite
      poet reminds me that a weed cannot be contained,
even in the hubris of this poem. So, I admit, I am
      often ashamed of how I can pass between several
towns without the practiced ritual of honoring one
      field with a stolen image. My wife points out the fire
-weed. &, like a child, I repeat *Fireweed,* without taking
      notice. Here, from where I am currently perched,

are entire fields purpled with fire. & my buddy, who

       has emerged from the doorsteps into the yard, is speaking

into the camera's beating heart to posit how *You*

       can eat this weed referring to a species of vegetation unlike

that which delivered him upstate. & tangential, perhaps,

       is how one species of plant might devour another.

& how one may facilitate another's growth. You see,

       the thing about fire is that my friend is now vegan.

A raw foodist to be exact. & my wife's uncle Jerry,

       who used to bring her dandelion jam throughout

the years of her youth, purchased his first suit

       to attend our wedding. I'm talking, years ago—

on an island where we watched the slow hands of lava

       seduce a flame that coursed down a hill's green back,

until all that was left was absence—which, yes,

       is a precursor to growth. &, upon this growth, I would

have sworn to you that every wild thing that bloomed

       was a flower. Which is absurdity, I know. My hubris

flaunting its purple head. The stuff of bees collecting

       in the calyx of fireweed like the curls of one's hair.

More than likely, Uncle Jerry is buried inside the fabric

       of his first suit—with the petals of something beautifully

wilted in his lapel. & listen to how I desire to say *fire*

       when there is no need. Speaking of summer, when the allure

of redwoods sheltered us from the burn with their

       leaves, we walked between laughter & astonishment:

Uncle Jerry, & his identifying every species of plant

       by their scientific root. Now, my own father is dying—

while I wish for a summer when I feared the bees

       who were too busy to fear me back. Today, I watch them

land & exit this poem. Because living is hard work.

       Especially, when every piece of legislation is meant

to uproot you. &, at the heart of every grass root,

       is a movement of bees fighting to keep. Which is a statement.

& believe me, I understand the effort it takes to show.

       & not explain. So, as a gesture of new growth, allow

me this one moment to re-catalogue *a tall showy wildflower*

       that grows from sea level to the subalpine zone. A member

of the Evening Primrose family, taxonomists previously included in

       the willowherb genus. Today, *it is now* home in *the Chamerion*

group. Which is code, yes, for *fireweed.* A wildflower known

       for its verse-like persistence. & by persistence I mean:

It is appropriate to begin   with a song.

I.

Though these poems defy the pastoral conventions of Western poetry, are they not pastorals?
Are these not meditations on nature? We find poems set in urban streets. Can these not be landscape poems?

Camille T. Dungy

Landscape

after William Carlos Williams

Our neighborhood of stolen bikes, backyards, & so

-called conditions of standard living (where nothing was much),

Papa would drive up, reverse, & parallel into his spot like the spot depends

on the smoothness of his return. Wednesdays upon

the red brick column we leaned, porch heavy & lethargic like a

scene to be duplicated the next week. I would eyeball the red

brick weighed between brothers. Brushstroke my hands over the worn flaws. & a wheel,

accompanied by other wheels, would always come to a halt whenever a child would barrow

across the one-way like he was tethered to a friend—or a loose ball glazed

in bacon grease & popcorn oil. Sometimes those headlights froze on a naked dime with

-out renaming a street, avenue, or lane, but often they did not. Rain

was the usual culprit fingered in a series of lineups. Valvoline & water,

the other that shot mothers out of starting blocks, Jackie-Joyner-Kersee beside

their child lying broken in the

road. From our red brick America, this was our rerun, our white

picket fence, our Wednesday evenings Papa made it home, jivin' he saw a man about a duck.

The Ghost of Johnnie Taylor Encourages the Lone Fledgling of a Robin to Jump and Reminds Himself That the First Love to Break His Heart Wasn't a Woman at All

Did I ever tell you about the time
I called out a man's name—

& my father never looked back?
Now, each time I take the stage

Momma asks: *Who do you think you are?*
I ask for the lights to be turned down.

(It's better that way for a man to live).
Until the only desire before me

                          is a void.
Pickin' cotton is hard on the feet.

So I learned to open my mouth wide
with one verse in the earth

& one   for the angel of the Lord.

Sometimes, in a spotlight, bright
as the North Star, a man can burn

the sweet of his sins. Or the way
can be as clear as lookin' into the red tip

of a cigarette. Baby, at the heart
of every song that answers to the body's

demands—beggin'. I mean a real deep
beggin'. Like an invitation to a soft bed

at the end of a cul-de-sac—is a prayer.
So can you blame me if I drank

from the well of echoes
like every city is my own to keep.

Listen, baby.
If I felt it. I sang it.

If I sang it. I've done it.
Our wings eventually take the flight

of our fathers'. What do you think
all this leavin'   is for?

Today

My father sits on a sofa not his own / in a home not his own / watching a television that is not his / My sister calls to tell me this / Perhaps to bring me comfort / Perhaps to comfort herself / Or in hopes / that I might pass the prognosis down the communication lines / to family members / waiting to hear news of our father / Who is frail / Has not been well for months / & no one can see him besides my sister / who texts me a photo of a man half his weight / in shoes twice his size / Apart from this / I know he is watching a Lakers game / reruns of Kobe Bryant / & I wonder / how much he remembers: / Will Kobe pump fake / evade two defenders / go for the lay-up / or the reverse dunk? / I don't want to ask / how long he will survive / not even to hear what he will say / Just the other day / it seems / I was under the hood of my first car / (a green Ford escort / given to me by a man who is like my father / but is not my father) / reattaching the battery cord / that kept it from firing like a disconnect in the synapses of the brain / when he approached my blindside / with the imperative I needed to hear / These days / they say / he repeats the same questions / replays the same words / like his father / but I had not noticed / This was how we spoke / This is the most we have spoken in years / All I hear is my father— / He asks me / *How's the weather?* / & I tell him / expecting to hear his laugh / I ask him / *How are you doing?* / & my father / is always / 60 degrees

Possible Titles for a Love Poem

I WAS ONLY A TEENAGER

        when I promised my mother
        with my first NBA pay stub
        I would build her a home

        A pact I never made with you my father

& YOU NEVER ASKED

        You were not 71 then as you are now & without
        your own plot of land—nor a gardener father

        nor one visit
        from meeting your oncologist

FRAIL AS WHAT A SOWER'S SEED COULD OFFER
        new earth

        & if
        it were possible
        to hold anything against you

MY FATHER

        there is still soil enough here
        to bury the hatchet
        measure a fallow—but

            THIS IS NO PLACE TO BURY A MAN

this is not how I
measure you father

WHEN YOU ARE MINE

nor is this how I measure the distance

wedged between you & my mother—nor

THE DECADES OF BLOOMING

the chrysanthemum callus:
the flower buds of your hands

but how you worked
lost seasons

IN A FIELD

to keep our rented home—a rented home

how you
rose early
to provide for us children

OF WILDFLOWERS

how you believed
just as hard as any
& so parked your company van

ANYWHERE IN THE CITY

where
your son was playing

(FORGIVE ME FATHER)

basketball

You Tellin' Me if My Grandmomma Was in the NBA Right Now She Would Be Okay?

Anfernee Hardaway's grandmomma nicknamed him *Pretty,*

      which she pronounced *Penny.* &, like a prophecy, pennies

clung to the back of his jersey sales ever since. & DJ Quik said,

      If it don't make dollas, it don't make sense. Which I also take to mean

If it don't make dollas, it don't make cents. & it would be

      a damn shame if I know more about Penny's grandmomma

than I know about my own. So, yes, I am a child who neglects.

      &, yes, I let two of my majestic palms die near the patio window.

From what, I do not know. Maybe their appetite became

      estranged from daylight. & I kept feeding them central air.

& I liked Penny, until his Orlando Magic defeated my Chicago

      Bulls in the Eastern Conference Semifinals. May of 1995.

In the year of our Lord. & see, the thing about a nickname

      is that it's not just a nickname. Like the time Aaron called me *CK.*

Cus, in '95, Kevin Blunt christened me with *Crisco Kid,*

      until it stuck. The same way he knighted Dookie with *Dookie.*

& can you imagine goin' through four years of high school

      bein' dubbed *the shit*? What I'm petitioning here is, it could work.

Or it could fail, miserably. Like the lunch period I went up

      for a dunk, & Aaron yelled out *Damn CK!* (which could be

mistaken for *crip killa).* & the hood in the heart of a YG

      propped up, cus he caught it as disrespect. & his set became more important than the highlight. & Aaron nearly died

      that day. & like the blacktop was stringing together a net worth

of copper bodies to fight in a new war, I said *Nah,*

      he ain't bangin'. My name's CK. & what I mean to say is,

Out of love, I made claim to what was not mine. So when MJ,

      on his first comeback tour, reentered the NBA on some

forty-five shit—he put the whole league on notice.

      & everyone but the Orlando Magic gave up the ghost.

& I thought, *Disrespect if y'all want. The arc, that is MJ's*

      fadeaway—is reenterin' its prime. & Penny might as well

have had a number 1 wit' a bullseye on his back. Cus,

      to be pretty, is to be pretty. To be a penny is to smell

your hand after you release a fist full of coins

      onto the counter of the liquor store, with enough cents

to cop some candy corn before the game. & perhaps,

      like my inner critic, you are low-key posted—lemon-faced

like: *& what does any of this got to do with your grandmother?*

      Mostly, it's her voice I remember. After the stroke,

how difficult it was for her to say my name.

      How, in 1996, my Chicago Bulls came back

& swept the Orlando Magic in the Eastern Conference Finals.

      & my grandmomma   was still alive.

Turnkey Sonnet #14: Trope of the Perfect Entertainer Getting His Flowers *or* My Attempt to Record Black Geographies into Song

feel   how   we'll   styl   ize   any   bona fide   city-   croon   to   bloom

in lieu   of   foxgloves.

One Side of an Interview with the Ghost of Johnnie Taylor Given by the Queen of a Humblebee Hive above His Grave

after Hanif Abdurraqib after Eve L. Ewing

J.T. :　It's not all what you think when you see the lawn thick with want—when
The man you know knows his work will bring him to his home again. The
Same home where he mows the grass that grows like it's here to be judge—

Caseworker—& instant hit to my back pocket. You hear the crowds give
Half-an-ear. That's all. & what I promise them? Nothin'. Believe me, you
Enter here the same way I do. But it's not yo' halls I walk down. Hear that?
Appearance is everything. &. Ain't. I. Green? Al taught me that. Listen, baby, dirty
Pathways make dirty shoes. & these alligatas ain't cheap. But it pays to look…
Every dance ain't free. & every hotel's booked. You hear the song, but you
Rarely get the music. Listen, baby, where do we go from here? Home? In May?

J.T. :　The sun, baby, ain't even gone down. Tomorrow's another sold-out stage. As
Over-packed as a night can get. Even my sweat got a name. You a drop in a well.

J.T. :　Keep yo' honey, honey. The night's on me. Yes, I can make a house a home. & put
Every two-step in its place. It only takes one glance to make a song. What's your
Excuse? Rhythm & Blues? Soul? Disco? Doo-wop? I've done 'em all. These money
Poplars are Monet's. My money don't grow on trees. Whether I close in

Hollywood or Memphis, it's all work. & it all works the same. I'ma open your
Ear so wide you gon' forget why you came here. Now. Ask me about my momma's
Ribs, baby. So I can say: *You look like a good cook. But can you keep yo' hands　　out my pocketbook?*

My Father Falls in Love for a Third Time and My Bill Is Five Hundred Dollas

circa 2002.
& I had a phone plan.

& my father was in need
of a number. Because

a young honey dip caught his eye.
& he was a working man.

With all his working parts.
& the plan had peak hours.

& limited minutes.
& we all know the song about

how *love can't wait*.
Or how we should *wait on love*.

& I can still remember loves
so fresh to the touch

they had monarch wings.
& I hesitated to be clothed

in moonlight.
I was *saving all my love*

for an audience of one.
& if the shower head

was my microphone.
& the tub was my stage.

Then my exit
was a curtain call.

& my father swore to me
that he had found a love

that cost him
nothin'.

Emmitt Smith Is Looking for a Wife so My Mother Writes Him a Letter

& Dallas is America's team

& it is some date

in late July

or perhaps just the 1990's

& my mother & father

have been divorced

for some years

which means

I am somewhere

between

then & now

in a tense that is future

perfect

but am nowhere

closer to showing you

what a father's absence does

when desire takes

the shape

of one

who is not my mother

& if it were not

for my brother

I would have plum forgot

how months before

their divorce

my mother removed the ring

from her hand

likely

with soap & water

Yes, We Wept at the Green Light and Held Up Traffic *or* "What Is Love? (Baby, Don't Hurt Me)"

is not my mother & father's song / but smoke follows beauty / & beauty is the birthplace of a heartache / I

pray / you never come to visit / & since every matter of the heart / leads / to a love track / best lost to memory

/ here I am again / among the conference room seating / surrounded by four walls of stale paint / & a beige

carpet / that looks as if it has held onto / every aching / that has fallen into the ground— / & to my best

recollection / this façade to my right / with its revolving door / holds behind it / an impossible love / &

to my left / is a painting clung to this rendition / which is about as inspirational as elevator music / & the

lawyer I don't know outside of his collared shirt / is the only one who enters & exits this grief / & he's tryin' to

sell me on a heart that splits two ways / after having tongued the same chorus / too long / & he peddles this

rhythm like a one-hitter-quitter / out the trunk of his car / & by this I mean / the only refrain that leads to

childhood / heartbreak— / so / I ask you— /

which heartbreak would you choose:

/ your father? / or / your mother? /

since I have been conditioned to believe / all black families survive / absent / of their fathers / listen / lost

loves / I did not choose my mother— / though I left with her that night / at a responsible age / when our

optics / (auditioning for brake lights) / mirrored the seconds / we held

The Ghost of My Grandmother Looks Out over a Baseball Diamond and Tells Her Daughter about a Man Coming Home

Sometimes you can see a season / bruisin' through an evenin' cloud
      Yo' daddy / runnin' into the house with a fist full / of cash

when the sun finally sets / You may call it / *turning over a new leaf*
      But I knew it for what it was / before I knew what it was

He had thrown in the rent / the baby / & the bathwater
      & went for broke / & sometimes the heart is a catcher's mitt

& life throws us a lemon / & we learn to make lemonade
      It threw him an orange / & he made a screwdriver with it

& sometimes the dealer threw in a wrench / & he'd bet the house
      toss in the kitchen sink / Yo' daddy you must understand

was a man of his time / During an era / where I'd smile through
      a pleasant breeze / from a *Colored Only* window

& a game of cards meant / for three months Momma had to go
      down south / Or it meant Daddy had three months rent

& yo' daddy had stories child / Lawd he could talk the sun down
      over a city with lily-white lips / & when he won

he'd enter the house like wind / Tell me to hide his cash
      some place he won't remember / Say / *Lena—*

don't let me near it / *no matter how hard I beg* / & he could beg
      & if that didn't work / he could swing / for the fence

Yes, I Beat Jason's High-Yellah Ass for Making Fun of My Pronunciation and Emancipation Was Really Not That Long Ago

When my father, along with his siblings, entered
into the city limits of St. Louis, he was a country
boy who had only known wooden homes built
by their owners. & railroad tracks with endless
fields headed north of somewhere. & I can still
remember turning ten in California. & putting
hands on a friend who'd ask me to say *hair*
one too many times. & what else can we do
when our lips brush up against *progress*—& some
utterance, most beloved, is sought—after having
gone missing? So what I desire most these days
are the kinds of stories that will carry me
into another summer. Meaning, the days when
my skin *burns* most bright. & the tragic thing
about language is how casually we use it. I say
burn, & you may think *a body lost to a forest.*
You may think *the hottest star—dying out.* I say
burn & it is a love track lost to passion.
An endless field of longing. Stories ringing
in the ear of each generation. It is a question
of passing. & how Big Momma Malinda Tony
lived 104 years to tell *her* daughter, who told *her*
grandchild about the day *her* mother saw Lincoln.

& how Malinda's husband was an indigenous man
with coal black *hair* when Lincoln arrived to their
town. & how she & how they waved as the train
set off. Leaving everyone's *hurr* blowing freely   in the wind.

My Father and I Drive to St. Louis for His Mother's Funeral and the Wildflowers

There is a story in a journey / a son takes / with his father / that circles back to a field /of flowers / that stays a field of flowers / only in name / & because our eyes pass them along a road / so / there is a point in a journey when all the years blur the same / Meaning / the details it took to get there / & the details it takes to get back— / & there is a point in a journey when a volta pivots inside a narrative / when a father turns the wheel over to his son / & this is the moment when a father releases his child / to the wind / & the boy learns to fail / or the boy learns to fly / & we desire shade from our oak trees / where the robins watch their nests / & sure / this could be a story about how a parent never rests / once his hands relinquish control / & my father never slept along the journey / (though / I'd seen him doze) / & we mostly ate fast food / & paused for gas / so / there is a point in the journey when the journey becomes a hill / a literal slope / somewhere between a field / & Texas / where our bodies enter a highpoint / & there is a tension / & / peripheral to a son / & / peripheral to a father / are likely flowers blowing in a wind / that could be from anywhere / & we could be anyone / & I could ask for anything / so there is a point in a journey where I become a magic lamp / & my father becomes a field of wildflowers / & the thing about a magic lamp is / how gently the hands tremble / once the wheels turn slowly onto the shoulder / so there is a point in the journey / where I pull off the road / & I am asked to exit my vehicle / as if I had a choice / so there is a point in the journey when the frame holds / & the hill stills / more or less its green / & the dandelions become a haven / for the bees to stuff their pockets / with gold / & / by this standard / my father can no longer be likened to a field / of wildflowers / & / the thing about a magic lamp / is / I only get three wishes / & my father is being cross-examined / as I make use of them all / so there is a point in a journey when / *who lives to tell the tale* / & / *from what point of view* / become central to the climax / & if the man toting the gun has a third-person limited / & if the plane in the sky has a god's point of view / I am all out of wishes / & the thing about a journey is / at some point it becomes a prayer / & what I mean is / *from this point on* / & the man with the gun is all about the math / & see— / what should be viewed as routine / does not start out that way / & what is likely to be believed / requires / neither of us / so / there is a point in a journey when it ends the way it begins / with that which appears different /

upon the surface / & the man toting the gun wants to know / if our stories corroborate / & to think / all of this came from my being / too relaxed / from allowing my foot to coast down a hill / while I mistook a field of dandelions to be a field of wildflowers / & that was my mistake / & the plane that was said to have calculated my duration / to distance (before the age of drones) / is not put to a vote / So there is a point in a journey when I return to the math / & I have never been one for arithmetic / so forgive me if my story does not add up / I leave this problem for you to resolve / since I know that you will work through my miscalculation / & the thing about a miscalculation / is how a journey could end / & the thing about a journey ending is / how easy it is to misfire / & what I mean is / how easy it is to begin with a field of flowers / & end / with no flowers at all

II.

With meaning so located, little wonder that American nature could not supply the imagination. If the object had to carry "storied" associations in order to resonate, it had to be connected to a remembered past of human events.

Larzer Ziff

Second Nature

In California where my brother filled a pot with hot water
& poured it out through the thousands of miniature squares
that make up the whole of a screen window which held
as expected securely to its square frame high above
the branches of a newly planted tree where I'd watch the birds
that I could not name alight & ascend leaving the branches
waving their freshly budded leaves as a gesture to a memory
that has returned only to fly again in the wind that blew pages
from a *Hustler* magazine into the air with stars covering
the most intimate parts of the regions I would come to associate
with desire but not before my brother & I observed there below
our second-floor apartment window a neighbor's kid digging
holes into what we thought was our dirt the tree for the moment
unbothered newly minted into a world in which we gathered
words like *mine* & *ours* & my brother & I thought we were
protecting our father's investment which was really not
our father's investment but an idea we believed meant *ownership*
where monthly dues figured more than the home my parents
purchased for twenty-seven thousand dollars in the 70's
& is still down to the dollar worth the same some fifty years later
where later the water my brother poured out from the screen
of the second-floor window found its target on top
of our neighbor's head the water now lukewarm no doubt
to the touch cooled by the air it encountered on its descent

& I of course can prove none of this because the head
which belonged to our neighbor who was really a small kid that
looked up at our second-floor window & said *This is not your land*
planted a sentence that no doubt stayed with me long enough
for me to share this memory with you & by *you* I mean *the silence*
I have come to expect & if this reframing were a trailer for a movie
where the two of us by some tolerance would eventually embrace
the other as lovers I swear to you there would be a deeply ingrained
tune playing at the end.

Blues Sonnet on What I Don't Have to Tell You in the Absence of Porches

with lines from Dawne Curry

Settings perform the same function as introductions.
                                        My grandmother preps the flames of her introduction.
Not only do settings inform readers and listeners

                                        when the tangent-string pulls, and there within, I muse
about the subject, the purpose, and point of view,
                                        like sticks she gathered, plain as words she'd never spoke,

they also capture the audience's attention. Settings
                                        like fields we children have never run through—such bearings
establish the tone that defines and illuminates speeches

                                        she'd give—had she given them in the place of shin splints,
autobiographical excerpts, and songs that document
                                        the boll weevil and vole, the twisting and turn of her hair,

the chair next to the fire like a bottle of good whiskey.
                                        You know everybody knows about Mississippi.

The Ghost of Johnnie Taylor, the Philosopher of Soul, Tells the City How He and Sam Cooke Left the Country, but the Country Never Left Them

A song in a field is worth the same as a song in a church. & I've tithed in both. &, at the age of six, I

Considered the lilies of the meadows the same as the meadow larks. & sunset, for me as a child, was
Heaven held in a gold tooth. How I do marvel at the way life greets us in the sliver of a thing. Born
Arrested is not the same as born under a restful night's sleep. I desire my country-count-of-sheep by
Name. & not by number. I wished to exit this earth glorious as perennials in spring: an encore in the
Garden which calls me back. A little dirt hurts nothin'. Nor do the roots of the Mississippi River
Envy the windows to which I cleave. Let me sing it plainly: *Baby—I believe—in you. You believe—in—*

Impatiens. How each can grow to light up a corner, to phase out any burden of proof. Proof? A
Song can build a road that outlines a city block. Listen, baby, land is land. My want of earth is little

Gone now. Was that not, in & of itself, proof? Pardon my candor if I have grown impatient. The tent
On my soil has passed since expired. Now, it's time to give it all back. It's been a long time comin' like
November's expression: *Come what may. Come what might.* Forgive me if I want what buds return. The
Night finds me guilty of such toils. It's a hard livin'. & I wish you only to grow sweet by the river.
A stone's throw from where I've made my bed in every heart. That's how I survive. Listen to how I've

Conversed with you like someone not turning in his grave. Like the dead don't sleep. What has been
Offspring of the tongue still is. Now, when you open yo' mouth, picture pure soul comin' out. Me. Runnin'.
My glide smooth as the first platinum plaque. See now, there I go again. Livin'. Baby, I wouldn't ever
Entice yo' love to stay, if leavin's all I got. Everyone gots to die to somethin'. I've been   ever since.

Surely, I Am Able to Write Poems Celebrating Grass and How the Blue in the Sky Can Flow Green or Red— Poems about Nature and Landscape but Whenever I Begin the Trees Wave Their Knotted Branches

&, in a town with no lynch laws, I study how the tulips tuck themselves in at night, but the bars remain open. &, isn't it funny how the same gown worn by your grandmother during your mother's birth could resemble the same gown you wear before your funeral? My grandmother had eleven children. Married a man who'd go to the corner store for butter & come back on a different date. So I ask you, would you rather have a man's presence every calendar month of a warless year, or one that does not come back broke? My grandfather had stories, & a pocket full of portraits where he'd stroke the faces of dead men. & the story goes—my grandfather died near his fifties. & anything black that survives half a century in this country is worthy of celebration (so I am praying for more time). A weaver is a bird who builds a nest that could outlive a storm. & though I thirst for more than what seems possible most days, I still drink of the river's water. & did I tell you the *how* of the weavers' nest? For love, they build for two days straight. Airlift long blades of grass & tie them to the base of a tree branch until the nest hangs there like a keloid. & for the love of a female, in the wooing year, a man will plunge his hands into a blaze of fire & erect grandeurs of smoke. My great grandmother did not approve of my grandfather at first, but after she witnessed the ash on his hands, what he was willing to unearth was less deniable. When the weaver's work is finished, he stands over what he has done & beats his wings. If a female arrives, she will inspect the nest. If it is found worthy, she will feed their offspring within it. If it is found wanting, something will be destroyed.

Epithalamium *or* I Attempt to Write the Poem That Whitman Did Not Write *or* Our Knees Bent in the Photo Just before We Jump the Broom

I.

I would have married you anywhere beneath the sun.

    It just so happened we were Hilo-side. How it rained

every day except the day that was ours. & what a sight

    from the road for every rearview that passed by. The lawn

a small pitch of earth. The tent, a cool shade. If it sprinkled,

    I did not notice. &, yes, while I did sweat, it was justified.

You were late. & had been early your entire life.

    The first wink at dawn. The lines rushed before the chorus.

What was I to expect? Birds of paradise? Plumeria? 'Awapuhi?

    The anthuriums' waxed doors? How the florist made them

to open when I thought hydrangeas would do. Banana leaves

    & an empty can. The coffee—long put to use. The island

wastes nothing. Like the heart. Your mother's blouse,

    a lavender orchid. The headwrap of my mother's too.

The Ghost of Johnnie Taylor Reflects on "Who's Making Love" and Believes Every Spring to Be a Metaphor for the Muse

At night she would toss rocks at my window

       that disturbed the dust   & left scars

like the nails of one's hands. & I would leave

       my room to unhinge the latch

leading to that which I swore   not to welcome.

       In any event   the act of opening

one's door to another's hunger   implies

       the absence of light.

Sometimes   the call of one's howl is the only

       distinction between predator   & prey.

& I have watched the gallop of a sheltered hound

       lose himself   across the intersection

of the busiest street   summoned by that

       which was not love.

In truth   a warm body is the source

of every song's demand.   Regardless

of how the bedsprings cry out. Or who or what

enters   the floral sheets.

I Will Not Escape without Leaving a Trail of Stars; Therefore, I Will Tell You How Spectacular You Are Under All This Light *or* I Want to Write a Song for You That I Will Not Complete Which Ends in Its Own Refrain *or* A Poem on How I Want

to spell *love* in the image of the spine's arch.

to speak with a guarded casualness.

that borders along the lines of. superstition.

i am not the last black man.

you'd ask me to be.

&. if. i. was. i'd want to be.

imaginative enough.

to let down my hair. in the absence of kin.

i understand what it means. to end

a line with *twitterpation*.

& because the woman i loved. brought home a man.

& my father placed our dead

dog in a box.

i lost. twice.

& so. i understand the intimacy. of keys.

the search for a lanyard.

whereupon. the bulk of its face.

is pressed. to a door's lock.

i mean to show you *loss.*

wherein. the mouth of the poem.

the words have gone missing.

& by *missing.* i mean.

what little we have had to hold.

& so.

i expect me. to corner myself. into a room.

to slap box. my shadow. into a closet.

to be a salve. to your tongue.

{chorus}:

Turnkey Sonnet #9: Trope of the Sexual Superman and How He Got His Rep *or*

scripted   into   d.w. griffith's   shoe   polish   i   acknowledge

why   imagination   ends   reconstruction   in   white   light.

The Ghosts of Frederick Douglass and W.E.B. Du Bois Collaborate to Write in Defense of Juxtaposition

You can see the light of the stars at night

only because of the darkness of space.

& so I take up every space & create these

parrot objects inside disparate rooms.

Furnished rooms. Each built by parallel

hands with doubled & conscious effort

to divide & subvert division. By longhand

I learned to usurp what is mine. By just

-ice veins & full throatedness. For sake of just

-ification (duality of reason) I'll try even

-ness—as if not from a dissimilar perch—

the bridge I built with my own hands

to get us here—to juxtapose my position—

as if it were not mine. Darlings of the court

the landscape is plain. Poplar Tree: Wide Lens:

Yard: & Popular Gardens—it arrives that

by the time this moment passes—the past

(to examine the bodies' sweet bloom)

my dears—will outlive us all. This condition.

This juxtaposition. This *object X object Y*

proximity to one another (to use visual optics)

has doubled out of focus. In your books

blinding white space serves as whole chapters

of history—not one lost but recentering

on a long blank gale. Circumnavigating

the globe. I have stood in contradictory

winds. Disproportionate & side by side—

juxtapositions—& I was not indifferent.

Now the years of my own ignorance burns.

I planted the sweet perfume of the oleander

at their word. To juxtapose is to lay one's

narrative next to the other's proof. & with it

contrasting effect. If I say *Jim Crow is alive & well*

you will preach the end of segregation.

If I speak *40 acres & a mule*—you will damn

Reconstruction—as I juxtapose postcards of

yourselves *with blood on the root & blood on the leaves:*

pastoral scenes—of two antithetical settings.

[John] Adams' Argument for the Defense: 3 – 4 December 1770 | The Ghost of Crispus Attucks Stands Outside the Old State House and Speaks for Himself

"Bailey "Saw the Molatto seven or eight minutes before the firing, at the head of twenty or thirty sailors in Corn-hill, and he had a large cordwood stick. So that this Attucks, by this testimony of Bailey compared with that of Andrew, and some others, appears to have undertaken to be the hero **of the night**; and to lead **this** army with banners, to form them in the **first place in Dock square, and** march them up to **King-street**, with their clubs; they **passed through** the main-street up to the Main-guard, in order to make the attack. If this w**as** not an unlawful assembly, there never was **one in the world**. Attucks with his myrmidons comes round Jackson's corner, **a**nd down to the party by the Sentry-box; when the soldiers pushed the people off, this **man** with his party cried, do not be **afraid of** them, **they** dare not **fire**, kill them! Kill them! Knock them over! And he tried to knock their brains out. It is plain the soldiers did not leave their station, but cried to the people, stand off: now to have this reinforcement **coming down under the command of** a stout Molatto fellow, whose very looks, was enough to terrify **any person, what had** not **the soldier**s **then to fear? He** had hardiness enough to fall in upon them, and **with one hand** took **hold of a bayonet**, and with the other knocked the man down: **T**his **was the behaviour** of Attucks;— to whose mad behaviour, in all probability, the dreadful carnage of that night, is chiefly to be ascribed. And it is in this manner, this town has been often treated; a Carr from Ireland, and an Attucks from Framingham, happening to be here, shall sally out upon their thoughtless enterprizes, at the head of such a rabble of Negroes, &c. as they can collect together, and then there are not wanting, persons to ascribe all their doings to the good people of the town.

Using the Laws of Motion to Explain Ferguson

from the Columbia Electronic Encyclopedia

1.   First Law

a body at rest tends to remain
            at rest
a body in motion tends to remain
            in motion
at a constant speed in a straight line

unless acted on
by an outside force

2.   Second Law

the acceleration *a* of a mass *m*
by an unbalanced force *F*

is directly proportional
            to the force

and inversely proportional to the mass
or *a* [knee-jerk reaction] = *F* [ired shots] / *m* [ichael brown]

3.   Third Law

for every action there is an equal
and opposite reaction

the total momentum of a system
        of bodies
not acted on by an external force
        remains constant
(see conservation laws in physics)

4.   [Limitations]

~~newton's laws of motion~~
~~together~~

~~with his laws of gravitation~~
~~provide a satisfactory basis~~

~~for the explanation~~
~~of motion~~

~~of everyday macroscopic objects~~
~~under everyday conditions~~
       however

when applied to extremely high speeds
or extremely small objects

~~newton's~~ laws
      break down

Working Title

A

    as in the time I was addressed after an evening of avenuing down the boulevard, minding my own scratch, knowing a simple whiff of anyone's smoke was hazardous: to sniff up any ol' tree standing buck-kneed like a display on a fractured sidewalk of someone's *You ain't from 'round hurr*, smiling through a chipped-tooth depression with the root of its tree bark like a toothpick home in the crevice of incisor & canine—was not wise. More like an *Ay,*

B,

    wasn't that the cat eyein' yo' girl? or *Ay, cuz, where you from?* because he noticed the red in my Cardinal's

cap,

    which would be coo' if I were in a gang or chasing after a pop fly. But, out here, it's either to live or

die

    like LA—or become a Padres fan. Or a type of Benedict Arnold schmoozing Blue Jays in Fenway Park. Which got me to thinking:

Everything must have started with a big bang.

    Someone had to throw out the first pitch. The first stick must have echoed off the first homerun that shattered a universe of windows. & left

fragments of

glass

    twinkling like tiny orbs in the rearview of my mother-in-law's mirror, blurring my vision. Or a disco ball. Or glitter in the glove of a singular Jackson. A singularity one might call *The '80s.* Someone had to throw out the first cowbell. The first haymaker

      that left the first glass jaw

in

      star-like daze: a

jab, then a

      right, then a *bang!* in the

kisser of

      someone who'd rather be hugged, than a head in

laurel, or

      a ring of stars hovering around someone else's good night. I didn't want to be either. Though I do admit I've been kicked in my jubilees once or twice. & I've felt a faint twinge in my gut whenever I strolled down the backstreets of someone else's salvation—where, with a homeboy, one is conflicted as to whether he should keep my jacket for himself as spoil, or alternate Mondays with his friend. So I escaped the valley of his

mind

      long enough to warrant a visitation. Which is precisely why this poem has a working title. Because what do you call a *bang* that has

not

      happened? An existential *bang?* A *bang* in theory? A theory that does not exist—like *In theory, he was . . . He appeared to be . . . He reached for . . . What was to me . . . What I perceived to be . . . A gun!* The theory of presumption, of opposition,

of opposites attracting. The singular *bang*: a hot & infinitely dense point whose eve brought forth *forth*—raised Cain,

perfectly—

so much so, *so on & so forth* became *in orderly fashion.* A quagmire

(quintessentially).

A theory in quasi-physics. Which means, if somehow you haven't yet discovered, I am quasi-knowledgeable about everything. Which makes me a master of nothing. Which is to say, *I know nothing,* only that I don't know enough to

render an explanation (if possible)

of why the *bang* in my adolescence watched me pass down the alleyway of a narrowing universe with his boy trailing behind while he ran to cut me off at the opening between two walls, where our eyes connected in

surprise,

finding there a fence—ten feet high—I would have missed nine times out of eight—had it not been for

the

sloth in their plan that aided my escape (in theory). Or (perhaps) later took the shape of another in his jacket (in an alternate universe). His blood mixing with soil. Red as a red bird: the crimson ring of my Cardinal's laurel, rendering the spoils

unsalvageable.

What I'm saying here is, without a working title, a poem could muddle meaning, confuse purpose, become vicious,

        or a

world-rocking

        super split from a singular form similar to a black hole. Which, after receiving a charge, is fired like a gunshot. Like an

x-ray revealing

        the shadow of a fragment in the back of another which could have been

your

        name (in theory). An all-black universe with stars circling in halo after a wild haymaker sent a body to the canvas, knees buckling *Good night* at best—at worse, a *bang!* into someone else's

zodiac.

Squire—The Outlaw! *19 July 1837* | The Legend of Bras-Coupé Speaks on the Creation of *Frankenstein; or, the Modern Prometheus*

This notorious black scoundrel was yesterday killed by a Spaniard in the swamp near the Bayou road. It will be **remember**ed by all our citizens that Squire was **the** negro who has so **long prowl**ed **about the** marshes in the **rear of the city**, a terror to the community, and for whose head a reward of two thousand dollars was offered some years ago. The life of this negro has been one of crime and total depravity. The annals of the city furnish records of his cruelty, crime and murder. He had killed several white men in this place before he fled to the swamp, and has up to the time of his death, eluded, with a dexterity worthy of a more educated villain, **all the searching efforts of Justice** to capture him. He has lived for the last three years an outlaw in the marshes in the rear of the city. Many years since he had his right arm shot off; he is said, notwithstanding this deprivation, to have been an excellent marksman, with but the use of his left **arm**. **Inur**ed by hardships and exposure to the climate, he has subsisted in the woods and carried on, until this time, his deeds of robbery and murder **with the most perfect impunity**—the marshes surrounding the city being almost impenetrable to our citizens. This demi-devil has for a long time ruled as the "Brigand of the Swamp." **A supposition has always found** believers **that** there was **an** encampment of outlaw **negro**es **near the city**, and that Squire **was** their leader. He was **a fiend in** human shape and has done much mischief in the way of decoying slaves to his camp, and in committing depredations upon the premises of those who live on the outskirts of the city. His destruction is hailed, by old and young, as a benefit to society.

…

About two o'clock yesterday his body was exhibited on the public square of the First Municipality. For the sake of example, two or three thousand slaves were encouraged to go and see it. Squire was so well known to the negroes of the city, it was thought it would have a salutary effect to let them gaze upon the outlaw and murderer as he lay bleeding and weltering in his [l]ore.

My Black Ash in the Sun Is Not a Phoenix

The orthopedic surgeon tells me

    after the surgery,

after seven stitches,

    after three nights in the hospital,

after the IV drip in the vein,

    after several treatments of antibiotics,

after the prescribed capsules,

    after ten days in a soft cast,

after having my stitches

    removed,

    I am more likely to have scar tissue

        because I am African American.

& I wonder if he wonders this beyond clinical fact.

    If somehow, he's been following the news.

Reading headlines. Doing his research.

Does he know

how many nights I've been planning

old tissue reform,

watching skin thicken beneath skin,

waiting new flesh to take?

Self-Portrait as *Yes* and *Amen*

I am beginning to notice your anthesis more. To explore my reflection

      at the face of your window. I am beginning to note

the turn of seasons like another year that has barely escaped. As for my father,

      he sleeps upon the hospital gurney. Which is to say that

he is conscious—but has yet to open his eyes. I am watching the young man

      who steered my father's bed on wheels into the room

where my father will be studied for the next week. I am told that when transplanting

      a crescendo of flowers, the procedure is delicate,

so note how the transference uproots, how the young man grabs one end

      of the sheet with his sturdy hands—as the CNAs,

my sister, brothers, & nephew gather to join in the chorus. Now, my father hovers

      from one resting place to be planted in another.

This is not how I have learned to identify the crocuses that arrive before

      it is officially spring. It is helpful to know they remain

in the same spot near the park-bench each equinox, no matter who or what

      arrives during the hour's turning. & while it is true that

some of us believe our father is dying, & some of us believe he will again bloom,

      it is still early. What is clear is that his dementia is budding.

& he is dehydrated. & malnourished. &, I want to convince myself, more than any

      spring, that he will pull through. That all he needs is time—

like any prayer

planted into a bed that

still calls *home* the earth (it inches above).

And Someone Said, *Those Poems Are Valid and Important and Good, but It's Hard to Constantly Be Fighting for an Inch; for That to Be One's Sole Mode of Artistic Expression*

& maybe Someone meant:

Every season is an inch	The flowers grow—yes?	& isn't it green how
Someone attaches themselves	to a front yard for	annuals
when perennials need only half	the work? Isn't it hard	to keep fighting
to keep bending forward into	all that topsoil	for that to be one's soul
purpose	? I mean if you are	to be buried—I mean if we are
to keep	going	like this—you may as well go quiet

After *Shut Up and Dribble*, a Three-Man Weave

& I thought to myself how *This is the Age of me being a man.*

  Growing my beard like a familiar phenomenon

    I have witnessed on the streets of Jerusalem. & beard kits

    are trending in every barbershop & Walmart across this country.

  & I attend this church, which is a kind of country club,

with uniforms who have served this country in one capacity

or another. & I, no doubt, watch the wrong news. & don the wrong

  view of Jesus' face. So, I admit, I find it difficult sometimes

    not to assume that my beard reminds my pastor of King James.

    From the city of angels. Who dons his beard in a more public space.

  & my pastor comes from a long line of clean-shaven chins.

Chips. Off the old block. & I am a churchgoer experimenting

with new-found growth. Like I have years past, when

     The Answer taught me to propagate several cornrows

          across the top of my dome, as if it were a faith-like gesture.

          A God-given fact that, if I kneeled at your altar of hardwood

like the harvest was plentiful & a strand of three cords not easily

broken—holy, I could live.

A One-Sided Conversation with Whitman Using His Words *or* A Sonnet Written on the Topic of Silence

You shall no longer take things at second and third hand.

    You should look through my eyes.

I perceive—after all—so many uttering tongues. Apart from

    the pulling & hauling stands what I am.

I smell the white roses sweetscented and glowing. I reach to the leafy

    lips and breathe the air and leave plenty

after me. It is you talking just as much as myself. I act as the tongue

    calling my name from flowerbeds—or vines

or tangled underbrush—the smells of sedgy grass by the shore—

    to a drudge of the cottonfields I lean.

This is the grass that grows wherever the land is. Noiselessly passing

    palmfuls out of their hearts and giving them to be mine.

My father—My beloved poet—you seem to look for something at my hand.

    I do not press my fingers across my *face.*

III.

palm prints fold around / the names of the things / seasons like skin

it is / about how we have learned to see ourselves. / it is about geography / and memory.

Lucille Clifton

Anti-Pastoral

My mother fixes me between her collarbone & ear

        likc she is fixing me between the knees of her lap.

                & I am small, & a child again. & she is aptly passing

down a lineage of stories I have never known. Stories

        I'd like you to hear. *My endeavor is never to keep you too long.*

                Which, I admit, could have been my grandmother's

phrase, who I have only known with a boll of white hair.

        I'm coming to it. But for now, allow me to reset the scene.

                For clarity purposes. My mother & I are on the phone.

Not one knee in my grandmother's field—white

        with the ripening of harvest that rubbed her fingers raw.

                & her mother's fingers wrong. Though I cannot say

for certain that I lingered long in her ear, nor stroked

        a hair upon her head. Worse than that, if I did, I cannot

                know if I have said anything that my mother had not passed

along. But I know for sure these hands have never

        known cotton sown, nor picked. Nor anything as white

                & light that could fit into a sack that, at the close of a hand, could weigh in at several hundred pounds (with children

      in tow). So, my grandmother took flight: A great murmur

           -ation of wings beating across the countryside into migration.

Allow me to say it bluntly: *I have stood all day in the sun's bright*

      -ness for no other reason than to darken my face. My hands fine

           as murder, whispering: *All of this, & none of this, is mine.*

If You Were to Ask Me the State of My Country, I Would Say

In the clear light that confuses everything,
         a tree grows as one might have grown
in the Garden of Eden. It started its wander
         like any tree in the world would: small,
significant, having a purpose, a desire to bud
         leaves. The neighbors call it an elm,
a Siberian elm, because some could see
         into Russia. Perhaps in strain or collusion.
But this is not the point. This is the light
         of the mind. Cold & planetary. The forest
of buoyancy that suffered Alexander,
         who from his true course turned the hands
of this telling to a tree-pull on a hill
         overlooking the icy river, and now,
the greenhouse is dark. Gone. And here
         must I remain as the storm-struck oak
leaned closer to the house.
         I say this   to be beautiful.
It is not the chambers of the heart which hold
         the affairs, or the tree, but all we know of history.
It is said they planted trees by the graves.
         In some narratives, the young girl throws
poisoned peas out the window. In some narratives,
         there is no such window.

Surely, I Am Able to Write Poems Celebrating Grass and How the Blue in the Sky Can Flow Green or Red—Poems about Nature and Landscape but Whenever I Begin the Trees Wave Their Knotted Branches

& there were days I'd request a new cereal box just so I could break its seal, to retrieve with the gift of my hands that which was buried deep inside. So yes, there is a point when a molly becomes an anecdote. When lint in the pockets becomes the center of one's earth. & what I mean is my grandmother arrived back to Mississippi like her leaving was a mistake. She stepped off the train like a million-dollar god with a two-cent paradise. & the toll that must have taken on her bones' pride. It takes less swagger to plant a harvest than it does bones to retrieve its crop. The one thing they can never call us is *lazy*. My aunt spends her retirement in the sun tending her petunias. My grandmother returned to a field of cotton with light pockets before she entered the earth. I prefer *creative* over *resourceful*. The homies that live by code of streetlight log more lunar cycles than the ones who patrol. Lazy is a whip. By which I mean, one who oversees a field gallops through the moisture that seeps from its glands, while the fieldhands are already ripe with enough perspiration to produce a second harvest. You see, the thing about my aunt's petunias is they demand all her attention. Deadheading is the act of keeping what is fleeting beautiful. &, after all that tending, the heads we pluck off go where we go to die. & since a little exercise is par for the course, & the course being that of life, my aunt feels safer coursing throughout her garden that she sprung forth from her hands than she does walking through her neighborhood in the suburbs. & the homie peddling ecstasy as a party drug shipped to him inside a cereal box by way of certified mail, is indebted to the rumble in his stomach. &, I'm not sayin' it's right. But I am sayin' something is wrong when a city demands we live this way. & I know cotton is not harvested until July, & October, in the northern regions of the Southern belt. & now that my relations are no longer under the full weight of the sun, all that clockwork beneath the threat of stroke has shifted. Now, machines plow these fields into the cool of night. & see how they called us lazy among the pastures that first blossomed with flowers, then budded into afros, bulb thick. Now flip that. If lazy is Lillie Mae among the cotton she trimmed slim in Jackson, then this poem is not about a season of returns.

Ars Poetica *or* American Pastoral as Opening Scene for a Micro-Documentary after Flipping the Script and Keeping the Darkness for Ourselves

//

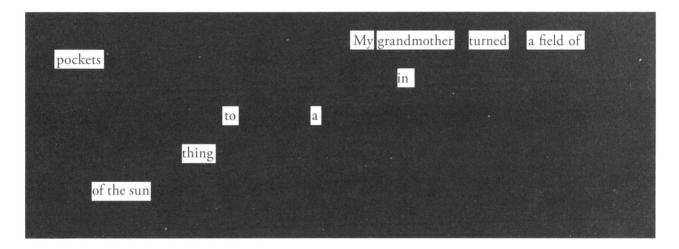

//

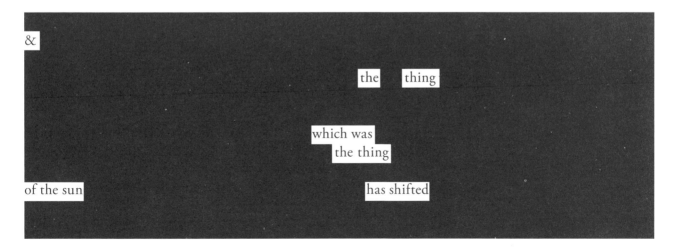

//

&

the seed

buried deep inside

the pocket

is

a

god

of

demand

//

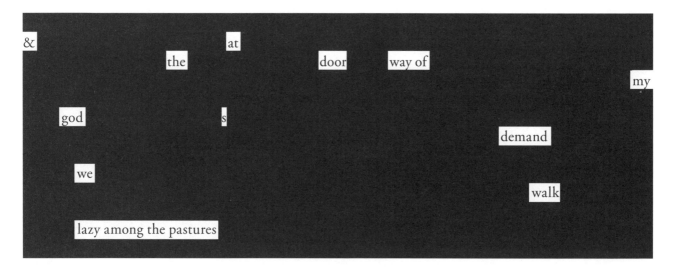

&

at

the

door

way of

my

god

s

demand

we

walk

lazy among the pastures

//

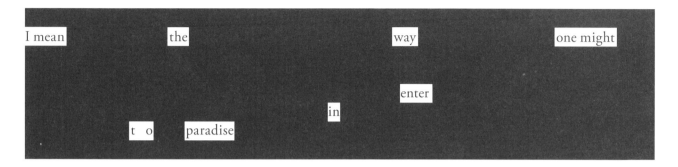

I mean the way one might

enter

in

t o paradise

//

You see the thing about

keeping

is

some flowers bud

into a

poem

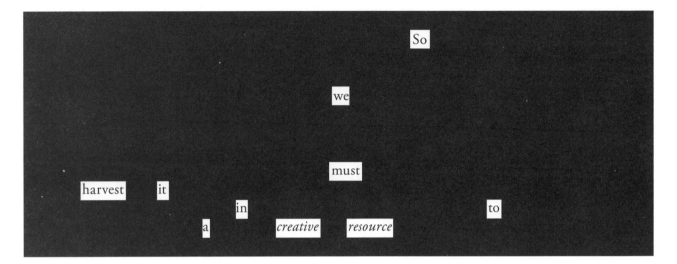

So
we
must
harvest it
in
a creative resource
to

And Someone Said, *Those Poems Are Valid and Important and Good, but It's Hard to Constantly Be Fighting for an Inch; for That to Be One's Sole Mode of Artistic Expression*

& maybe what Someone means is   to show precise moments.   Like when my nieces

         & nephews   line themselves up,   turn their backs against a white wall

like their sole purpose is to be   an em dash: a smudge-point

         just above the crown of their heads.   Exact inches.

& maybe I mean to show   how inches do not grow sunflower   from a top hat.

         Yes. Nothing magical appears from a flowerpot   without precise intentions.

& maybe Someone needs to know that.   To know how it takes a seed,   for example.

         It takes care.   It takes luck.   It takes a fight

to be free from a season of no other escapes: the bully in third grade   who circles

         like the forces of nature.   Only, this season will end.   My nieces & nephews

will grow.   They will peel their heads   from the walls of their youth   like old paint,

         like a split-leaf philodendron.   Maybe what Someone needs to see   is proof.

Poem of Remorse Ending in Reparations

A stone's throw from where Elisha
performed his second miracle, you

will find pilgrims gathered under
a tree for shade. A tree I could have

climbed easily in my youth. Like
the single oak in the backyard

of three police visits before the age
of nine. The same tree I watched

my brother wrap a rope around
his neck & hang there like oak.

More so an oak than the sycamore
Zacchaeus climbed in a city

9,000 years old. At the age of twenty
-three, I knew everything. I told my

mother, *History doesn't matter.* Now,
I throw no stones. I arrived at that

fact after being saved a third time.
In a mega church. I raised my hand

when no one was looking.
The invitation came. Then the root

of the stage. I took Jesus in before
the invitation was given. But the man,

who did not close his eyes, told me
to go down. Who told Zacchaeus

to climb that sycamore when Jesus
arrived? My brother swung from that

oak like a tire swing. Strange fruit.
After I was evicted from the oak branch,

I went into my feelings early. I sobbed
too much to turn around. I threw stones

across the street because, across the street,
they threw stones back. When I lifted

a brick up, the size of this poem,
the children my age booked for cover.

Sometimes words shatter like that. Like
the back of an Opel's window. & you

stand there holding the smoking gun.
My brother's legs kicked & dangled.

His eyes licked the back of his lids.
& I stood there in wonder. 9,000 years

Jericho remained an inhabited city.
I repeated what I was at the foot

of the stage. That man never closed his
eyes. Zacchaeus, in awe of the moment,

was a nation—waiting to be saved.
When the rope broke, my brother

poured out like a drink offering. Later,
I split his brow. This was my second

visitation. The brick laid groundwork
for the first. The Opel owner's son

broke into our home, stole the VCR.
Therefore, this poem is a patchwork

of memory. The brick, an eye for an eye.
When Zacchaeus climbed down, he met

with Jesus. I dug into my seat again.
History doesn't matter, I told my mother.

How can you say that? she replied.
This poem is a tumbling—someone falling.

My brother survived as a feline would.
Bosnia. Afghanistan. I prayed

he would make it back alive. He came back.
Retired. Months later, like Lt. Nazario,

he became a match for a match. My brother,
nearly the same shade. Sometimes history

wears a black face, a black face—blackface,
at any rate—it repeats itself.

It rhymes. It throws stones at a glass house.
Shatters windows. Moves on from a single-

tree home to an apartment with no shade.
Momma, I was wrong. We invite Jesus in.

Survival is our history. My brother
given back. Flailing to his knees.

Zacchaeus emptying himself.
A sycamore. In the sun.

The Ghost of Johnnie Taylor Kicks Game to a Paper Birch about the Economics of a Recording Contract Signed on What Is Otherwise a Piece of Wood

The rule of thumb is to list your demands

at their doorstep. Even when you are the door. & the key to unlock

the words behind the rhythm's two-step. Observe if you will how they press

my breath into the vinyl's warm mouth. & a yearning climbs out. & a label cuts the check.

Now check how the disc jockey reads my fortune inside the rings like a stump's palm. Now

everything begins dying at a consumer rate.   How am I not complicit in your going?

I wish to find you how they say the one   doing the soul searching finds them

-selves in a forest. & you'd be saved. The way a *Whereas* emancipates. You see the trouble

in my logic? Knowing that in any responsible age the limitations of one's breath

has everything to do with the events that have transpired. Allow me a second

attempt to express how I know this is a backwards love: I tell the wood

-nymph he is guilty for cutting down trees. & behold

I am   the mothafucka.

Ars Poetica *or* Self-Portrait Beginning with a Haiku before Shaking the Polaroid into Image and Keeping the Darkness for Ourselves

//

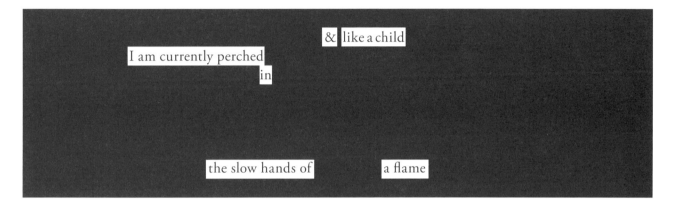

//

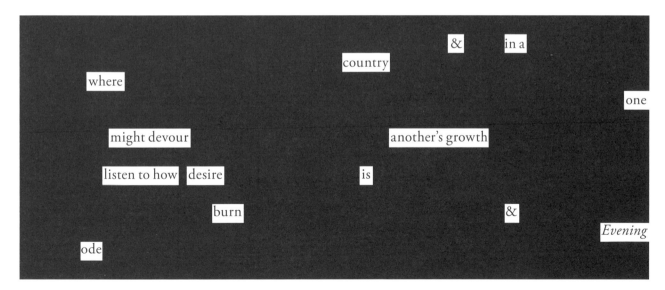

//

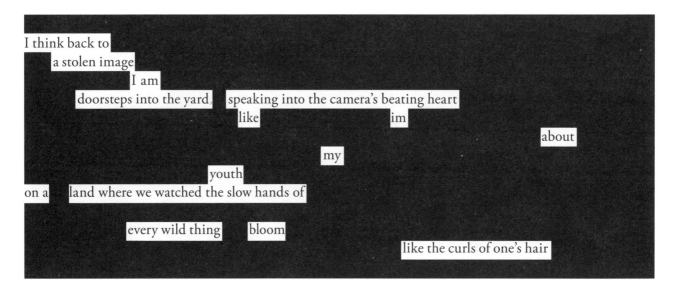

I think back to
a stolen image
I am
doorsteps into the yard,   speaking into the camera's beating heart
like   im
about
my
youth
on a   land where we watched the slow hands of

every wild thing   bloom

like the curls of one's hair

//

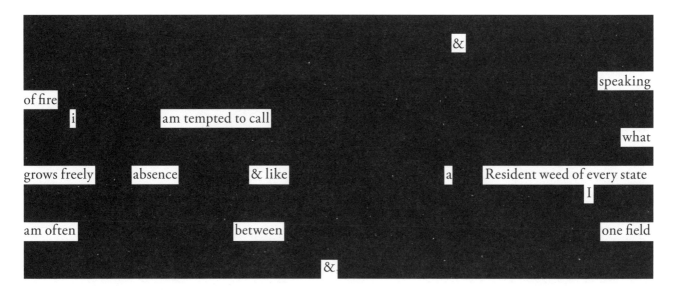

&

speaking

of fire
i   am tempted to call

what

grows freely   absence   & like   a   Resident weed of every state
I

am often   between   one field

&

another   &   the   thing   is

throughout the years

I   have

sworn to you that every wild thing that bloomed was

likely

buried inside the fabric of his first suit

Michael Brown as My Father *or* Michael Brown as My Grandfather *or* Michael Brown as My Father and My Grandfather *or* All Three as an Old Man

He entered the park's archway   hands withered like the leaves of November shuffling

beneath his feet   finding & losing themselves like the memory of one who pauses

every   few steps   to remark upon the buildings   that had once been trees

& searches the sun until he finds himself   lost & lingering like a stray to the public

bench   where he removes his cap balances his cane on his leg   & examines the faces

of strangers as one would   a map   When I found him there he had already begun

speaking of rivers   going on about the weather   seasons & the earth's axial tilt

how it was perfect like the curve of his Cardinal's cap or the hem of the city's ballroom dress

He complimented the sun   & spoke skylines   over the moon's obsession

with shooting stars   how he whispered   *dark matter*   into the celestial ear

of open space   & how the shadow of the earth passes over a smile   as a light wind

lifting silver leaves   like embers   from their place   & he spoke of how

the same happiness can remind a man of sorrow & how both   reminded him

of Evening   in the garden   & the first dance   they had ever danced

Epithalamium *or* I Attempt to Write the Poem That Whitman Did Not Write *or* Our Knees Bent in the Photo Just Before We Jump the Broom

II.

A lavender orchid, the headwrap of my mother's too bloomed

      in the sun. &, if it would have rained, I would have

unplugged the cords. I would have removed the heels from your feet.

      I would have peeled my pant legs from the sea

of my ankles, as though there were green shores. The grass, the same

      dampness between our toes. I would have held the train

of your garment until you were sheltered from the hostas of heaven.

      I would have watched you through the dewfall

as my hands recede from your dress like the crest of a wave.

      I would have waved at the faces as the clouds passed by—

by & bye to our un-wedded selves. The seasons before I had loved you.

      I love you. I say it plainly. There is always something left to be said:

The African American sonnet speaker is often doubly divided, arguing internally, politically, and aesthetically.

Hollis Robbins

[Or]...you might tell me something about the dandelion & how it is not a flower itself but a plant made up of several small flowers at its crown & lord knows I have been called by what I look like more than I have been called by what I actually am & I wish to return the favor for the purpose of this exercise.

Hanif Abdurraqib

Interview with a Field Guitar's Twelve Strings Speaking on Themselves and When Johnnie Made It

turnkey sonnet 1. // *we thought:*
misunderstood   mahogany   wood—   we   string   a   rustlin' may
into   your   new   splendor.   all day long   we work that song.

turnkey sonnet 2. // *we say:*
we work that song   good.   we   should. erry body   plantin'&pickin'. dey
pickin'   a   blue   chor'   to   underscore   "good-as-gon'."

turnkey sonnet 3. // *we thought:*
good-as-gon'.   & befo' long—   hollywood.   as far as the eye can see.   what's da likelihood   j.t.
makin' headway?   the damnedest thing   dey   eva knew: buckboar'   to   billboar'.

turnkey sonnet 4. // *we say:*
billboar'   (no. 23) song!   "jody got yo' gurl & gon'"'!   so far so good,   we   would   agree.
seen it comin'.   erry dog has his day—   moon-shinin',   same kinder way   home-brew-new-   liquor   do.

turnkey sonnet 5. // *we thought*
dew   pour'.   befo' long,   a star was bo'n.   make good,   j.t.,   make good.   we
taught'em errythin' 'round dis hyuh way.   pickin'&croonin'.   sweat&sway.   rhythm&blue   splendor.

turnkey sonnet 6. // *we say:*
splendor.   unto   it pour.   on   & on.   when the gittin' is good.   believe-you-me,   we could
see   sumthin'   out dat way   comin'.   what mo' can we say?   —

turnkey sonnet 7. // *we thought:*
—   folklore, hoodoo,   or—   on   the day he was bo'n,   what would
we be? what could   we   jaw-jackin'   say: "listen,   rome wasn't built in a day?"

turnkey sonnet 8. // *we say:*
rome wasn't built in a day.   make do—   or—   string sum kinder new   chor'.   make the coffee strong.
work that song   good,   yah see. erryone could.   we   singin': pick-a-bale-of-cotton-pick-a-bale-a-day. listen—

turnkey sonnet 9. //
listen, say,   you   tenor? you   counna-tenor?   we got this hyunh song… (gon'   be jus' as good):
since-my-baby-dun-left-me…(i mean—if she could, she would). since-my-baby-dun-left-me…(meanin': she dun gon' away).

turnkey sonnet 10. // *we say:*
she dun gon' away   singin'. where there's a will, there's a way. true   for   who?
befor' long   she'd be gon'   fo' good. maybe   hollywood.   maybe   plantin'&pickin'.

turnkey sonnet 11. // *we thought*
plantin'&pickin' erry which way, singin'&gleanin' the day away,   would do   for   a few.
or   headstrong   passion   could   be   jus' as good,   yah see.

turnkey sonnet 12. //
yah see, sharecroppin',   dis hyunh way, savin' for a rainy day, accrue   bales galore.   unto
prices soar.   landlor'&loan.   same ol' song.   dogwood to the nth degree. we made do wit' what we could.

turnkey sonnet 13. // *we say:*
we made do wit' what we could.   to what degree? plantin'? labor-day   pickin'? slavin' our way   through
dirt-poor? we givin' you   more   song— (right or wrong)   than we should. johnnie was good as we'd eva be.

turnkey sonnet 14. // *we thought:*
johnnie was good as we'd eva be.   made it far as he could.   what about we? hootin'&hollerin'. all-day   croppin'.
no pay. you   'member feelin' blue?   'member "ain't-no-sunshine-when-she-gon'?"   this time, we gon' fo' good.

the key: Johnnie Taylor's Ghost Writer Speaks

the way i enter this poem, is the way i exit this page. black. & misunderstood.

have i left my first love only to return with a '68 excalibur (with its mahogany

earthen-face)—so my people may rest their feet without damagin' the wood?

song-seeker, here i am again, celebrating life as if a parade. we—may i say, "we"?—

only occasion what we have survived since birth. dr. bland, save the guitar's string.

nina, i'm gon' need you to sing along. aretha, would you please be my nurse? i'm a

neighborhood away from bein' rebo'n. all this stompin'. folks turnin' their rustlin'

eternity into hollow graves. i can hear that. the sound of muddy waters. & may.

the beat of black soil. we sowin' somethin' good. i can feel it in my bones. we into

creation, ain't we? & who can do it better than us? so riotous to bring you along. your

rhythm's better than mine. soul on the page. called it a cage once. tried to make it new.

only, i'm over that now. give me sunrise in the mornin'. heat of days. all that splendor.

we want what was sown back. can i say that? well, there it is. we've been all-day-long

noddin' between starshine & clay, rhyme & reason—just so we can say: *we-work-that-song.*

Q & A

—Do you have a fear of losing people?
I once rustled moonlight underneath the blanket
& threatened to keep it. I unwrapped it slowly
like sand loosed by waves, a child with one present
come Christmas morning.

>*—Do you feel that being black makes you a target?*
>If shooting holes into darkness was not a sport,
>then each glow, each bend & arc, each reach
>& fiery flicker of stellar assortment would be a lie—

—Who did you vote for?
All I wanted were bodies back.

>*—Why do black people run from the police?*
>The concrete is hot. These are new shoes.
>As sons & daughters of Mercury, we are
>partial to wind sprints, Julys & Junes.

—Slavery was such a long time ago. Why can't you just get over it?
(Sisyphuses. Gluttons for punishment,
you'd joke.) Because some of us swam
to the sea's depth, told us this secret:
(   )

>*—Michael Brown is in so many of your poems. Did you know him?*
>I often viewed the Arch's bend over a small piece of St. Louis
>like it owned the city. I, in my school bus, passed—never able
>to connect both ends.

—Who is Icarus to you?
A canary under the heels of antelope. A Pegasus without wings.

—What have you learned from protest?
I'm in love with the sound of *freedom*: the way the top teeth
sink into the bottom lip, the way the tongue hovers in suspense
before bouncing suddenly to the roof of a mouth like a mallet
striking a lever, the puck rising to toll the bell, the last consonant
ending   in a kiss.

—What do you hope to accomplish by writing these poems?
I hope to release a hummingbird from the palm of my hand.
Watch it fly off on little wings.

Notes

I became acquainted with the prefatory quote, "Everything that happened to me involved music. It was part of every day life, as automatic as breathing," by Nina Simone through a Google search. I stumbled upon *The New York Times Style Magazine* and the article "The Artists Turning Nina Simone's Childhood Home into a Creative Destination" authored by Adam Bradley and published on 16 March 2022. Bradley cites Simone's 1992 autobiography, *I Put a Spell on You*, and it is from this text that Simone's words derive.

My interest in Johnnie Taylor began when my mother mailed me a family reunion pamphlet that she received during the summer of 1980. The second page of the family reunion pamphlet featured a photo of Johnnie Taylor followed by the titles of a few of his hit songs. The paragraph concludes with "He is Our Star of the Family. Look for Johnnie at a Family Reunion in Detroit or Cleveland next time it's held at Cleveland or Detroit." Taylor was first signed to Sam Cooke's record label, and Cooke co-wrote Taylor's first single "Rome Wasn't Built in a Day." Throughout the collection, I include Johnnie Taylor persona poems. The epigraph, "I do believe that something went wrong somewhere. I'm asking what's come all over me. I've changed, I've been changed. Let me tell you something about myself," cites Taylor's songs "What About My Love" and "Testify (I Wanna)."

"A Poem Ending with a Strambotto wherein I Include an Extra Line That Is Myself *or* A Poem in which I Name the Flower" would not have existed without the prompting of Nancy Lord. The final stanza of the poem gestures to the strambotto. The strambotto is an eight-line stanza that was sung by Sicilian peasants and appropriated by Giacomo da Lentino, "the senior poet in the Sicilian School of court poetry" and one of fourteen notaries working in the thirteenth-century court of Frederick II. According to Phillis Levin's *The Penguin Book of the Sonnet: 500 Years of a Classic Tradition in English,* da Lentino expanded the strambotto's eight-line structure into what we now know as the fourteen-line sonnet. The latter half of the title contains an echo of Hanif Abdurraqib's title, "A Poem in which I Name the Bird," which is included in his collection of verse: *A Fortune for Your Disaster*, a book I return to often and with gratitude. The italicized lines of the ultimate stanza comes from the Forest Service United States Department of Agriculture's website: https://www.fs.usda.gov/wildflowers/plant-of-the-week/chamerion_angustifolium.shtml.

The sectional quote, "Though these poems defy the pastoral conventions of Western poetry, are they not pastorals? Are these not meditations on nature? We find poems set in urban streets. Can these not be landscape poems?" comes from Camille T. Dungy's introductory essay titled "The Nature of African American Poetry" in her anthology *Black Nature: Four Centuries of African American Nature Poetry.*

"Landscape" is a golden shovel that would not exist without the innovation of Terrence Hayes and the words from William Carlos Williams's poem "The Red Wheelbarrow." The final word of Williams' poem ("chickens") is altered to fit a phrase that my father used often: "I went / I'm going to see a man about a duck."

"You Tellin' Me if My Grandmomma Was in the NBA Right Now She Would Be Okay?" is a verse from Kanye West's "Roses" on his album *Late Registration*.

"Turnkey Sonnet #14: Trope of the Perfect Entertainer Getting His Flowers *or* My Attempt to Record Black Geographies into Song" would not exist without Ronald L. Jackson II's monograph *Scripting the Black Masculine Body: Identity, Discourse, and Racial Politics in Popular Media*. This poem is one of two autonomous turnkey sonnets. The "turnkey" is a horizontal sonnet with a Shakespearean rhyming pattern. Here is an example of the turnkey sonnet with its Shakespearean rhyming pattern:

scripted		*into*	*d.w. griffith's*		*shoe*	*polish*		*i*	*acknowledge*
a		*b*	*a*		*b*	*c*		*d*	*c*

why	*imagination*	*ends*		*reconstruction*		*in*	*white*		*light.*
d	*e*	*f*		*e*		*f*	*g*		*g*

"One Side of an Interview with the Ghost of Johnnie Taylor Given by the Queen of a Humblebee Hive above His Grave" contains structural echoes of Hanif Abdurraqib's "One Side of an Interview with a Ghost of Marvin Gaye," which is itself after Eve L. Ewing's poem, "Excerpts from an Interview with Metta World Peace, a.k.a. Ron Artest, a.k.a. the Panda's Friend" published in *Electric Arches*. This Johnnie Taylor persona poem is an acrostic golden shovel containing the title of and lyrics from his hit song "It's Cheaper to Keep Her."

"Yes, I Beat Jason's High-Yellah Ass for Making Fun of My Pronunciation and Emancipation Was Really Not That Long Ago" remembers some of the women in my patrilineal lineage. My ancestor, Mary Knox, is estimated to have lived from 1834 to 1875. She would live to experience the very brief era of Reconstruction. Her daughter, Melinda Toney (est. 1850-1954), referenced in the poem, was born during the antebellum period. Both were alive to experience their emancipation from this particular US-American system. Melinda

Toney's daughter Mary Jane (1895 – 1981), the mother of my grandmother Carrie (Jackson) Ballard (1925 – 2003), shared with her children and grandchildren about the time her mother (Melinda Toney) saw Abraham Lincoln. I am in full gratitude to William Ballard, Annette Ballard, and Olleye (Ballard) Conely, for their work to keep our family narratives alive and accessible.

The sectional epigraph from Larzer Ziff comes from Ziff's introductory essay to Ralph Waldo Emerson's *Nature and Selected Essays.*

"Blues Sonnet on What I Don't Have to Tell You in the Absence of Porches" would not exist without Dawne Curry's essay, "'Through the Doors of Return:' Paul Robeson and Miriam Makeba's 'Migration' to Africa," in *New Frontiers in the Study of the Global African Diaspora: Between Uncharted Themes and Alternative Representations.*

"The Ghost of Johnnie Taylor, the Philosopher of Soul, Tells the City How He and Sam Cooke Left the Country, but the Country Never Left Them" is an acrostic golden shovel which includes the title and lyrics from Sam Cooke's classic "A Change Is Gonna Come." In his 1999 text *What the Music Said: Black Popular Music and Black Public Culture,* Mark Anthony Neal addresses the corporate censorship of Black cultural production. Neal writes: "when Sam Cooke's 'A Change Is Gonna Come' was released posthumously in the spring of 1965, the verse containing the lyrics, 'I go to the movies and I go downtown, somebody keeps telling me, don't hang around' was deleted for fear of offending Cooke's white listeners in the South. The recording would not appear in its original context for another twenty years" (51-52).

"Surely, I Am Able to Write Poems Celebrating Grass and How the Blue in the Sky Can Flow Green or Red—Poems about Nature and Landscape but Whenever I Begin the Trees Wave Their Knotted Branches" comes from Lucille Clifton's poem, "[surely i am able to write poems]" which is included in *The Collected Poems of Lucille Clifton 1965-2010.* This title appears twice throughout this collection.

"Epithalamium *or* I Attempt to Write the Poem That Whitman Did Not Write *or* Our Knees Bent in the Photo Just Before We Jump the Broom" is in conversation with Walt Whitman via Ed Folsom. In his essay, "Lucifer and Ethiopia: Whitman, Race, and Poetics before the Civil War and After," Ed Folsom writes: "…in Whitman's work[,] the poet creates no black characters, not a hint of a representation that offers a place or role for the freed slaves in reconstructed America. He toys with the idea of writing a 'Poem of the Black Person,' complete with 'the sentiments of a sweeping, surrounding, shielding, protection of the blacks,' but the poem never materializes. He thinks of writing a 'Poem of Remorse' in which he would 'look back to the times when [he] thought others—slaves—the ignorant—so much inferior to [him]self / To have so much less right." My goal was to engage with this quote. My attempt was to write the poems that Whitman did not write.

"The Ghost of Johnnie Taylor Reflects on 'Who's Making Love' and Believes Every Spring to Be a Metaphor for the Muse" references Johnnie Taylor's hit song "Who's Making Love."

"The Ghosts of Frederick Douglass and W.E.B. Du Bois Collaborate to Write in Defense of Juxtaposition" contains a reference to Abel Meeropol's song "Strange Fruit" sung by Billie Holiday. The italics here come from the definition of juxtaposition found on Grammarly's website addressing this question: "What Is Juxtaposition?"

"[John] Adams' Argument for the Defense: 3 – 4 December 1770 | The Ghost of Crispus Attucks Stands Outside the Old State House and Speaks for Himself" emerged after I learned about John Adams' defense of the British soldiers who shot and killed Crispus Attucks during the Boston Massacre. I was struck by how closely the rhetoric of John Adams resembles that of those made by the legal defense for law enforcement officers who face murder charges for using deadly force, in particular, against persons of color. The text in gray comes directly from "Adams' Argument for the Defense: 3–4 December 1770" as maintained on the site *Founders Online*, within the National Archives, https://founders.archives.gov/documents/Adams/05-03-02-0001-0004-0016. The original source resides within *The Adams Papers*, Legal Papers of John Adams, vol. 3, *Cases 63 and 64: The Boston Massacre Trials*, ed. L. Kinvin Wroth and Hiller B. Zobel. Cambridge, MA: Harvard University Press, 1965, pp. 242–270.

"Squire—The Outlaw! *19 July 1837* | The Legend of Bras-Coupé Speaks on the Creation of *Frankenstein; or, the Modern Prometheus*" emerged after I learned about Bras-Coupé through my wife's research. Bryan Wagner's article in *Representations* titled "Disarmed and Dangerous: The Strange Career of Bras-Coupé" provides an in-depth analysis that is further expanded upon in Wagner's later monograph *The Life and Legend of Bras-Coupé: The Fugitive Slave Who Fought the Law, Ruled the Swamp, Danced at Congo Square, Invented Jazz, and Died for Love*. The text in gray comes directly from *The New Orleans Picayune*, a local newspaper that published this article that echoes the same rhetoric and mythological monster-making found in contemporary testimonies that aim to justify the murder of Black persons. I believe that it also important to note the 2020 *Washington Post* article "They Lost the Civil War and Fled to Brazil. Their Descendants Refuse to Take Down the Confederate Flag," by Terrence McCoy, which chronicles how up to 20,000 US-American confederates left the US with their enslaved persons and moved to Brazil so they could continue the practice of enslavement, accessible at https://www.washingtonpost.com/world/the_americas/brazil-confederate-flag-civil-war-americana-santa-barbara/2020/07/11/1e8a7c84-bec4-11ea-b4f6-cb39cd8940fb_story.html.

The New Orleans Picayune was one of the Southern periodicals to provide commentary on the benefits of expatriating for plantation-based profits; one such article, titled "From South America" was published on 7 December 1865: https://www.newspapers.com/image/25562082/?match=1&terms=brazil%20immigration.

In "After *Shut Up and Dribble,* a Three-Man Weave," the italicized portion of this title comes from the Fox News host, Laura Ingraham, who directed her imperative "Shut up and dribble" at NBA athlete LeBron James for publicly voicing his desires for social justice.

"A One-Sided Conversation with Whitman Using His Words *or* A Sonnet Written on the Topic of Silence" is a cento. The lines come from Walt Whitman's *Leaves of Grass*.

The sectional epigraph contains lines from Lucille Clifton's poems "in which i consider the fortunate deaf" and "the river between us." These poems are both published in *The Collected Poems of Lucille Clifton 1965-2010* published by BOA Editions, Ltd.

"If You Were to Ask Me the State of My Country, I Would Say" would not exist without a writing prompt provided by Don Rearden. The cento emerged after searching for poems that reference trees on the Poetry Foundation's online platform. It contains lines taken from poems written by Samuel Taylor Coleridge, Tory Dent, James L. Dickey, Landis Everson, Jessica Greenbaum, Allen Grossman, Lisa Grove, Freya Manfred, Robert Morgan, Elise Paschen, Muriel Rukeyser, Louis Simpson, and C. Davis Young.

"Ars Poetica *or* American Pastoral as Opening Scene for a Micro-Documentary after Flipping the Script and Keeping the Darkness for Ourselves" would not exist without the guiding structure of torrin a. greathouse's "Burning Haibun" included in their collection *Wound from the Mouth of a Wound*. The words for this poem are taken from "Surely, I Am Able to Write Poems Celebrating Grass and How the Blue in the Sky Can Flow Green or Red—Poems about Nature and Landscape but Whenever I Begin the Trees Wave Their Knotted Branches," a poem located in the third section of this collection.

"Ars Poetica *or* Self-Portrait Beginning with a Haiku before Shaking the Polaroid into Image and Keeping the Darkness for Ourselves," too, would not exist without the guiding structure of torrin a. greathouse's "Burning Haibun." The words for this poem are taken from "A Poem Ending with a Strambotto wherein I Include an Extra Line That Is Myself *or* A Poem in Which I Name the Flower" which is the prefatory poem for this collection.

The sectional quote by Hollis Robbins comes from Robbins's monograph *Forms of Contention: Influence and the African American Sonnet Tradition.*

The sectional quote by Hanif Abdurraqib comes from Abdurraqib's poem "How Can Black People Write about Flowers at a Time Like This" in *A Fortune for Your Disaster.*

"Interview with a Field Guitar's Twelve Strings Speaking on Themselves and When Johnnie Made It" reflects a sonnet crown. A sonnet crown consists of repeated lines that connect the preceding sonnets to the subsequent sonnets. The turnkey connects the preceding horizontal sonnets to the subsequent horizontal sonnets as they turn.

Here, for example, are the turnkey sonnets with their Shakespearean rhyming patterns explicitly identified, either using single words or common word phrases:

turnkey sonnet 1. // *we thought:*

misunderstood	*mahogany*	*wood—*	*we*	*string*	*a*	*rustlin'*	*may*
a	*b*	*a*	*b*	*c*	*d*	*c*	*d*

into	*your*	*new*	*splendor.*	*all day long*	***we work that song.***
e	*f*	*e*	*f*	*g*	*g*

turnkey sonnet 2. // *we say:*

we work that song	*good.*	*we*	*should.*	*erry body*	*plantin'&pickin'. dey*	
g	*a*	*b*	*a*	*b*	*c*	*d*

pickin'	*a*	*blue*	*chor'*	*to*	*underscore*	***"good-as-gon'."***
c	*d*	*e*	*f*	*e*	*f*	*g*

"the key: Johnnie Taylor's Ghost Writer Speaks" is the fifteenth turnkey sonnet that completes the crown, as the acrostic letters read "THE SONNET CROWN" vertically. A sonnet crown consists of repeated lines that connect the preceding sonnets to the subsequent sonnets. The turnkey connects the preceding horizontal sonnets to the subsequent horizontal sonnets as they turn—linking the chain of sonnets together—while also allowing each sonnet to exist autonomously like the couplets of a ghazal. This fifteenth sonnet is labeled "the key" since the first couplet of the horizontal turnkey sonnet (*misunderstood mahogany wood—we string a rustlin' may into your new splendor. all day long we work that song*) can be read vertically since it is a golden shovel. The Shakespearean rhyming pattern, or golden shovel, in the fifteenth sonnet acts as a key that can be inserted and turned horizontally—thus, unlocking and/or revealing the rhyming pattern (which, in this case, follows an English or Shakespearean order). The term "key" also doubles as a nod to the musicality of the sonnet itself. The phrase "starshine & clay" is quoted from Lucille Clifton's poem "[won't you celebrate with me?]" included in *The Collected Poems of Lucille Clifton 1965-2010* published by BOA Editions, Ltd.

In the following "Acknowledgments," I quote from Lucille Clifton's poem "speaking of loss" also included in *The Collected Poems of Lucille Clifton 1965-2010* published by BOA Editions, Ltd.

Acknowledgments

My gratitude to the editors who not only provided a platform for, in many cases, the earlier versions of the poems included in this collection, but who have also been a source of encouragement.

The Atlantic: "The Ghost of Johnnie Taylor Reflects on 'Who's Making Love' and Believes Every Spring to Be a Metaphor or the Muse" (published as "The Ghost of Johnnie Taylor Reflects");

Lunch Ticket: "Q & A";

Michigan Quarterly Review: "Epithalamium *or* I Attempt to Write the Poem That Whitman Did Not Write *or* Our Knees Bent in the Photo Just Before We Jump the Broom";

The Missouri Review: "A One-Sided Conversation with Whitman Using His Words *or* A Sonnet Written on the Topic of Silence," "A Poem Ending with a Strambotto wherein I Include an Extra Line that Is Myself or A Poem in which I Name the Flower," "The Ghost of Frederick Douglass and W.E.B. Du Bois Collaborate to Write in Defense of Juxtaposition," "The Ghost of Johnnie Taylor Encourages the Lone Fledgling of a Robin to Jump and Reminds Himself That the First Love to Break His Heart Wasn't a Woman at All," "The Ghost of Johnnie Taylor Kicks Game to a Paper Birch about the Economics of a Recording Contract Signed on What Is Otherwise a Piece of Wood," and "Yes, I Beat Jason's High-Yellah Ass for Making Fun of My Pronunciation and Emancipation Was Really Not That Long Ago";

Narrative: "Working Title";

Nebraska Quarterly: "My Black Ash in the Sun Is Not a Phoenix";

Obsidian: Literature & Arts in the African Diaspora: "You Tellin' Me If My Grandmomma Was in the NBA Right Now She Would Be Okay?";

Oxford Poetry: "The Ghost of Johnnie Taylor, the Philosopher of Soul, Tells the City How He and Sam Cooke Left the Country, but the Country Never Left Them," and "the key: Johnnie Taylor's Ghost Writer Speaks";

Pittsburgh Poetry Review: "Using the Laws of Motion to Explain Ferguson";

Poetry Northwest: "And Someone Said, *Those Poems Are Valid and Important and Good, but It's Hard to Constantly Be Fighting for an Inch; for That to Be One's Sole Mode of Artistic Expression* (1)," "And Someone Said, *Those Poems Are Valid and Important and Good, but It's Hard to Constantly Be Fighting for an Inch; for That to Be One's Sole Mode of Artistic Expression* (2)," and "Anti-Pastoral";

Puerto del Sol: "My Black Ash in the Sun Is Not a Phoenix";

Rattle: "If You Were to Ask Me the State of My Country, I Would Say";

Ruminate: "Today";

Subnivean: "Possible Titles for a Love Poem";

Terrain.org: "Ars Poetica *or* American Pastoral as Opening Scene for a Micro-Documentary After
    Flipping the Script and Keeping the Darkness for Ourselves," and "Surely, I Am Able to Write
    Poems Celebrating Grass and How the Blue in the Sky Can Flow Green or Red—Poems about
    Nature and Landscape but Whenever I Begin the Trees Wave Their Knotted Branches";

The Tishman Review: "Landscape" (published as "Golden Shovel");

Verse Daily: "If You Were to Ask Me the State of My Country, I Would Say" (published as "If You Were to
    Ask Me the State of My Country…").

The poem "My Father and I Drive to St. Louis for His Mother's Funeral and the Wildflowers" (published as
"My Father and I Drive to St. Louis for His Mother's Funeral") was a joint recipient of a Bridport Poetry
Prize and published in the *Bridport Prize 2022 Anthology* (UK).

"My Father and I Drive to St. Louis for His Mother's Funeral and the Wildflowers" was also featured on
The Slowdown.

The poem "Q & A" is included in the *New York Quarterly*'s anthology *Without a Doubt*.

"A Poem Ending with a Strambotto wherein I Include an Extra Line that Is Myself *or* A Poem in which I
Name the Flower" is published in *A Literary Field Guide to Alaska* by Mountaineers Press.

"Landscape" (published as "Golden Shovel"), "Michael Brown as My Father *or* Michael Brown as My
Grandfather *or* Michael Brown as My Father and My Grandfather *or* All Three as an Old Man" (published
as "A Love Poem"), and "Using the Laws of Motion to Explain Ferguson," appeared in the chapbook *Flight*,
winner of the Sunken Garden Poetry Prize, published by Tupelo Press in 2018.

*

I am imperfect, traveling along this road of (un)learning and sense-making. I have failed and will,
undoubtably, continue to fail with my words. As one raised in the United States, I have been complicit in
my own erasure and the erasure of others' true and lived experiences. It has taken me years to understand
this. I have consciously or unconsciously participated in many blindnesses, and it may take me a lifetime,
if ever, to work toward seeing.

Thank you first to the good folks at BOA Editions, Ltd.—Peter Conners, Justine Alfano, Benjamin Thompson, Sandy Knight, among others—for your wisdom and your guidance, for believing in *Second Nature*, and for ushering the book into existence. Thank you for your humble beginnings as a small press and for the important role that you fulfill in American poetry today.

*

My gratitude to:

Matthew Shenoda for not only your generous reading of these poems, but for your care with and faith in this collection. Thank you for your words and for the important work that you do.

Lucille Clifton whose writings continue to find a home in the works of so many others—whom I have never met and yet feel pages of gratitude and indebtedness, but, alas, "I am left with plain hands and / nothing to give you but poems."

A. Poulin Jr. for kickstarting the BOA tradition wherein established poets introduce the press's readership to new poets and their first collections—for his poetry, his literary service, and the community he founded that continues to flourish.

*

Cristina Rivera Garza and Ross Gay remind us: Writing is not an act of solitude.

It is impossible for me to have written any of these poems without the help of those whose writing has been a gift and a guide: Hanif Abdurraqib, Jericho Brown, Kwame Dawes, Michael Kleber-Diggs, Rita Dove, Camille T. Dungy, Eve L. Ewing, Vievee Francis, Ross Gay, Terrance Hayes, Sean Hill, Major Jackson, Tyehimba Jess, A. Van Jordan, J. Drew Lanham, Natasha Trethewey, Quincy Troupe, Danez Smith, and Tracy K. Smith to name but a few.

Truly this gathering of poems would not have taken shape without Hanif Abdurraqib's *A Fortune for Your Disaster*. My indebtedness to you for supplying the blueprint and for showing me the many possibilities that are available within a single collection.

*

Elizabeth Bradfield for seeing many of these poems in their rawest forms and for responding to my sporadic emails with honesty and care.

Anne Caston for introducing me to the poems of Lucille Clifton and for sharing stories of your friendship with her throughout our time together.

Linda McCarriston, our fairy godmother, for your generosity, friendship, continued love and support, and for the many ways in which you have worked behind the scenes to provide for us an example of theory in praxis. How we look forward to wonderful summers with you on your back deck.

Zack Rogow for introducing me to a fellow St. Louis native, Quincy Troupe, through your anthology *The Face of Poetry,* and for your *Advice for Writers* blog that continues to impact the way I engage with various poetic forms.

*

Stephen Buhler, Pete Capuano, Joy Castro, Dawne Curry, Jeannette Jones, Gregory Rutledge, Ng'ang'a Wahu-Mūchiri, for your passion and instruction.

Stephen Behrendt for sharing your poems and scholarship with Tara and myself and for your many kindnesses.

Kwame Dawes for conspiring to provide space, opportunities, and resources for us students—and for your poetry, mentorship, delightful humor, and hospitality.

Ken Price for welcoming me into the Archives—for sharing your knowledge and resources pertaining to Walt Whitman and for your commitment to troubling US-American mythologies.

Hope Wabuke for your manuscript workshop that jumpstarted this collection by providing me with eyes to see, and for modeling the many ways in which we may engage the text.

Stacey Waite for the amazingness that you do behind the scenes and for being a relentless encourager.

Sandy Petrulionis and Diane Whitley Grote for the opportunity to participate as an NEH Summer Scholar at the 2022 National Endowment for the Humanities' Summer Institute in Concord, Massachusetts. Thank you for allowing me to take part in "Transcendentalism and Social Reform: Activism and Community Engagement in the Age of Thoreau." This opportunity was and is of great value to me.

My cohort and friends who are too many to name in this brief space that we create for acknowledging one another, I ask you to please forgive me for not naming you all here, but I would be remiss if I did not thank you for setting the bar and for providing inspiration throughout our graduate experience. I consider myself blessed to have shared in the creation of beautiful memories in the places and years that we have gathered together. You are cherished.

*

Aliki Barnstone for your heart and friendship and poetry. We thrive because of your generosity.

Major Jackson for your encouragement and continued dedication to introducing new and established poets and their poems to many audiences—and as I once again reflect upon your question—Yes. It did change my life.

*

My continued gratitude to my family through marriage—for your love and support, for summer Christmases and birthdays, and for providing space to work on projects that seem to have no end-date.

My love and gratitude to my family for keeping our historical narratives alive by sharing them with each generation. Many of the poems included here would not have been possible without each familial carrier and lineal mile marker which includes Melinda Toney, Mary Jane Jackson, Ollye Ballard Conley, Annette Ballard, Thornton Ballard, William Ballard, and Joseph Ragland—Samuella Johnson, Lillie Hogan, and Rosa Ballard to name but a few.

My love to my beautiful family who are presently in Alabama and Mississippi and to those who have emerged out of Alabama and Mississippi into the locations where they now settle. May we continue to gather to share stories of our ancestors and preserve not only our familial history but the history of place.

My father and my mother and sisters and brothers who I love with all that I have. Thank you. Thank you. Thank you.

My wife—how can I ever say enough? I would not have entered my first poetry class if it were not for you. Thank you for reading through this collection with a critical eye and thank you for approaching the hundred-and-thirty-first reading as if it were the first. You are my heart.

To the Most High.

About the Author

Chaun Ballard is a doctoral student of English at the University of Nebraska-Lincoln, an affiliate editor for *Alaska Quarterly Review*, an assistant poetry editor for *Prairie Schooner*, an assistant poetry editor for *Terrain.org*, and a faculty member of Alaska Pacific University's Low-Residency MFA Program. Ballard is the author of *Flight*, which received the 2018 Sunken Garden Poetry Prize and is published by Tupelo Press. His poems have appeared in *The Atlantic, The Missouri Review, Narrative Magazine, The New York Times*, *Oxford Poetry*, *Poetry Northwest*, and other literary magazines.

BOA Editions, Ltd. A. Poulin, Jr. New Poets of America Series

Colophon

BOA Editions, Ltd., a not-for-profit publisher of poetry and other literary works, fosters readership and appreciation of contemporary literature. By identifying, cultivating, and publishing both new and established poets and selecting authors of unique literary talent, BOA brings high-quality literature to the public.

Support for this effort comes from the sale of its publications, grant funding, and private donations.

*

The publication of this book is made possible, in part, by the special support of the following individuals:

Anonymous

Angela Bonazinga & Catherine Lewis

Ralph Black & Susan Murphy

Chris Dahl,
in honor of Chuck Hertrick

David Fraher,
in memory of A. Poulin Jr.

Bonnie Garner

Robert L. Giron

James Hale

Peg Heminway

Grant Holcomb

Teresa D. Johnson

Nora A. Jones

Joe & Dale Klein

Deena Linett

Barbara Lovenheim,
in memory of John Lovenheim

Joe McElveney

Daniel M. Meyers,
in honor of J. Shepard Skiff

Boo Poulin,
in memory of A. Poulin Jr.

Deborah Ronnen

John H. Schultz

Sue Stewart,
in memory of Steve Raymond

Benjamin Thompson,
in memory of Lyn Erickson

Lee Upton

William Waddell & Linda Rubel